Time-Honored Norwegian Reci[pes]
Adapted to the American Kitchen
by
Sigrid Marstrander & Erna Oleson Xan
revised mini-edition

Editors: Dorothy Crum, Maureen Patterson, Joan Liffring-Zug[
Melinda Bradnan, Julie Eisele, Miriam Canter, and Connie Sch[
Drawings by Diane Heusinkveld

Illustrations from the collections at Vesterheim Norwegian-American Museum, D[

Penfield Books

Acknowledgments

When he read *Wisconsin My Home,* Dr. Marion Nelson, former director of Vesterheim, thought Erna Oleson Xan's writing style wonderful. He contacted her at her home in Birmingham, Alabama, to see if she would compile a special cookbook for the museum. Mrs. Xan accepted the offer and requested that her good friend Sigrid Marstrander, a wonderful Norwegian cook, participate, too. *Time-Honored Norwegian Recipes* is the result of their friendship and collaboration. Both authors lived good and graceful lives well into their 90s.

This edition is possible thanks to the Vesterheim Museum staff: Janet Blohm Pultz, director, and David Wright, Tova Brandt, Carol Hasvold, and Charles Langton. For information about the museum, write: Vesterheim, PO Box 379, 523 West Water Street, Decorah, Iowa 52101, or visit its website at www.vesterheim.org.

ISBN 1-932043-27-6   ©2004 Vesterheim Norwegian-American Museum, Decorah, Iowa
First Edition 1974. Revised Edition 1990. Revised Mini-edition 2004.   www.penfieldbooks.com

Contents

Cover Photographs

Front cover: Spouted tankard, painted by Herbrand Sata, Hallingdal, Norway, 1804.

Back cover: Plate with rosemaling in free Os and Hallingdal styles painted by Per Lysne (1880–1947), Stoughton, Wisconsin, ca. 1935. Inscription translates: "The smorgasbord is on the table—help yourself!"

Both objects are in the Luther College Collection at Vesterheim Norwegian-American Museum, Decorah, Iowa. Vesterheim is noted for its collection of rosemaling and also its extensive folk art classes.

The Authors

Erna Oleson Xan wrote: "In writing this book, Sigrid and I want to thank our children, the 'green leaves and fruit' of our lives, for their love and support. Without them we would be lone trees in a winter field. My family is daughter Dixie and her husband Thomas Bullock, and grandchildren Kathryn and Scott Ellis. . . . As for help in writing the stories, I leaned on my two lifetime champions. First is Dixie, who started me into story-telling when she was about three. Pounding on my knees with her small fists, she would demand, 'Not wead, TELL!' . . . My other literary comrade was my sister, Henrietta Bear. . . . Fascinated with words, she had a newspaper column called 'The King's English,' and sold magazine articles. We wove into each other's thoughts like the warp and woof of a garment. In this present book, we worked by long distance telephone or face-to-face. She brought up many a happy memory.

continued

"Sigrid's delicious Norwegian recipes came out of very old cookbooks which she carried around the world, making a home for her husband Henning and son Jan. Born in Trondheim, Norway. . . . home of the renowned Trondheim Technical Institute. . . . Sigrid became assistant and cartographer to one of the greatest geologists of the day, Professor J.H.L. Vogt. . . . Professor Vogt was so dependent and grateful for Sigrid's work that he arranged for her to be decorated with 'The Star of Nidaros.' . . . It had never before been given to a woman.

"...Henning received both Master's and Doctor's degrees in Mining Engineering and Economic Geology. His dissertation, for which he also received 'The Star of Nidaros,' won praise in four nations. . . . For thirty years, [Sigrid] and Henning traveled to many countries by boat, train, car, and plane, staying two to four years at a time." **Note:** *When Henning was sent to the coal mines in Birmingham, Alabama, Sigrid and Erna Xan met at last, and became "sisters" for life.*

Norway: Notable Facts

- Norway ranks high in quantities of fish taken from the sea.
- Norway's coast is 15,000 miles long.
- By 1900, a total of 900,000 Norwegians had immigrated to America, a number greater than the population of Norway at the time.
- In Tromsø, from May 20 to July 23, the sun never sets.
- Norway is as far north as Alaska, but is warmer because of the Gulf Stream.
- Since 1905, when Norway gained freedom from Sweden, the king's right to veto legislation has never been used.
- Norway has 150,000 lakes and 50,000 islands.
- The map of Norway has been likened to a giant fish, its tail in the north, its mouth in the south (Oslo).

The Girl from Wisconsin

by Erna Oleson Xan

Just as Henning Marstrander asked Sigrid if she would follow him anywhere in the world . . . John asked me the same question. But I, less adventuresome than Sigrid, replied, "John, dear, I will follow you anywhere, but don't you dare ask me to go to the Arctic or the desert!"

John and I could never get over our meeting in Chicago. Born 6,000 miles away in Greece, he had come to America to attend Kalamazoo College, which was right across Lake Michigan from Waupaca (Wisconsin) high school where I went to school. Upon graduation, John went back to France to fight in World War I. . . . How was it that, one day in 1921, we met in that vast city? Whose lovely plan was this? On New Year's Day, 1921, coming into Chicago to begin a new job . . . I engaged a room at a certain Eleanor Club for Girls, where three of John's older friends lived. . . . The friends made slick attempts to get us together. It didn't work. Three weeks later, he saw me alone and said to himself, "There's my wife!". . . Our courtship was fun and we found things to celebrate all our lives. . . . John's last position was at Howard College (now Samford University) in Birmingham, Alabama, where for 24 years he was Professor and Head of the Chemistry Department. . . . John became famous for the number and accomplishments of his chemistry majors, and he received a national award. His students also initiated a college scholarship in his honor.

Erna Oleson Xan earned a master's degree in creative writing from the University of Michigan. Mrs. Xan's books are: Wisconsin My Home, Home for Good *(the story of her childhood on a Wisconsin farm), and* Time-Honored Norwegian Recipes. *She wrote for the* Birmingham News *for eight years, and was an adviser and reviewer for the* Christian Family Bookshelf.

Time-Honored Notes
By Erna Oleson Xan

Summary
Some things (foodstuffs) you may think are overdone. One is almonds. These are imported, but when cookie- and cake-baking time comes, Norwegians must have their almonds. Another is parsley. During the sunlit Norwegian summers, this green is grown in abundance. In winter, some raise it in a pot in the deep window-sill. Home-grown root vegetables are kept in the cellar. Almost everything fresh, like lettuce and tomatoes, is imported from warmer climates. The use of parsley must have contributed much to the health in the long dark winter months.

Eggs were scarce in Norway. Eggs were eaten usually only on Sunday morning, otherwise saved for baking. Chickens are still expensive in Norway, but there are plenty of fish, lambs, pigs, and cows. The old recipes were heavy with butter and cream. Rye, oats, and barley were the most common grains. Most wheat had to be imported, as was corn for animal food.

The cookbooks that Sigrid carried around the world held favorite recipes still used in Norway. Because the measurements in these books followed the metric system, our problem was to translate to the English cups and spoonfuls. The credit for the recipes goes entirely to Sigrid; my task was to adapt them to the American kitchen.

My mother, Thurine Oleson, used to say, "Bidden Food is as Good as Eaten." It means: "The honor is in the asking." So we bid you to come and eat, and do not forget our dear old Norwegian table prayer, "I Jesu Navn."

I Jesu Navn

I Jesu navn går vi til bords,
Å spise, drikke på dit ord.
Deg, Gud til aere, oss til gavn,
Så får vi mat i Jesu navn.

In Jesus' name we take our place
To eat and drink upon Thy grace.
To Thy honor and our gain,
We take our food in Jesus' Name.

Grandma Was Frugal

Excerpts from an article by Henrietta Oleson Bear, sister of Erna Oleson Xan. Mrs. Bear was married to the late Fred Bear, noted archer and big game hunter. Mr. Bear was the founder and chairman of the Bear Archery Company of Gainesville, Florida, home of the Fred Bear Museum and its wildlife displays.

In the early 1900s, I spent most of my school vacations with my grandparents in Winneconne, Wisconsin. Coming from a family of seven children, I loved these vacations. I received my grandparents' total affection, whereas at home I had to share the love and attention of our parents with all my sisters and brothers. On the other hand, at home we enjoyed delicious meals, while at Grandma's the food, though wholesome, was often very plain.

continued

In this scrupulous Norwegian household, there were two sets of dishes. One was of heavy ironstone, plain white and so heavy I could hardly lift the plates. These were for everyday use. The other set was daintier with an all-over pattern of brown leaves and azalea-like flowers. These dishes were kept in the yellow pine corner cupboard in the best sitting room and were used only when we had company. This was quite often, however, because so many of our relatives and friends came regularly from the village of Winchester to shop. They brought baskets of eggs and cream from their farms and sat down to Grandma's noon dinners. . . . We either had fried pork and milk gravy with boiled potatoes and carrots, or fried fish and fried potatoes with pickled beets. These menus were bolstered by homemade bread with butter and jelly. For dessert we had some of the white cake Grandma baked every Saturday. And coffee, of course.

The big dining-sitting room was heated by an iron cookstove. On all but the hottest days of summer, it was used to cook the food, boil the coffee, and heat the water. . . .

On the large back lot, Grandpa operated a veritable truck garden. To the left of the path were neat rows of vegetables—potatoes, onions, and carrots. There were no tomatoes, for he firmly believed that tomatoes were "poison." On the right of the path, he planted berry bushes—raspberries, currants, and gooseberries, as well as a healthy strawberry bed. In addition, there was a lovely grape arbor near the house where the vines hung heavy with grapes.

Nothing was ever wasted in this household. Potatoes, carrots, and cabbage were stored in the little black cellar under the pantry. . . . Grandpa arranged onions to dry for the winter. We seldom ate berries fresh from the bushes, since cream was saved for butter and cooking. Cream soured in thunderstorms, but was put to good use in the

15

continued

cookies. The berries, cooked in very light syrup, were put up in quart jars and stored in a separate pantry where the temperature was just right for keeping food without refrigeration. These glass jars of "sauce" accompanied every "company" meal throughout the year.

Grapes were not stored. We often had a bowlful in the middle of the oilcloth-covered table. But grapes spoiled rapidly and drew flies, so this was discouraged. . . . To prevent waste, Grandma cooked some of them into juice, which was brought from the cellar for callers.

Sometimes Aunt Julia came home from Ironwood, Michigan, for a visit. These visits were not the happiest times for her parents. Aunt Julia crimped her hair with a curling iron heated in the chimney of the dresser lamp. She ran up dressmaking bills, and spent far more for groceries than was customary in this household. She scoffed at her mother's Spartan ways and took over much of the baking. No more watery egg-white frostings now. Julia knew how to boil sugar and milk and make fancy fillings between the layers, instead of Grandma's jelly. She skimmed sweet cream from the milk and poured it over rich puddings. She used real butter in the cookies. When friends or relatives from Winchester brought gifts of pork or beef that Grandma could stretch for several meals, Julia cooked it all at once. We lived high during her visits.

Julia arrived with a barrel of empty glass jars and returned with jars filled with cooked fruits and berries. Grandpa paid the freight. Grandma furnished the sugar, not outwardly complaining, but full of wonder at the extravagance of her daughter.

In Grandma's category of sins, nothing surpassed that of wasting food unless it was breaking the Sabbath. . . .

Those years of Grandma's cooking were responsible, I suppose, for my unfaltering acceptance of food to this day. I can eat anything, cooked any way, at any time.

Porridges and Soups

The surface of this 1927 soup tureen is covered with repoussé birds and acanthus designs.

Vesterheim: Luther College Collection, Gift of Maihaugen Museum

Trondheim Fruit Soup *(Trondhjemsuppe)*

A delicious luncheon or supper dish with bread and butter or as a dinner dessert.

2 quarts water
1/2 cup uncooked rice
1 cup seedless raisins
1 teaspoon flour

3/4 cup half-and-half cream
Juice of 1/2 lemon
1/2 cup raspberry or strawberry juice
(canned or fresh)

Use a thick-bottomed kettle. Bring water to a boil; add rice, stirring occasionally. Cook for 1/2 hour, add raisins, and cook another 15 minutes. Make a paste of the flour and a little cream. Add rest of the cream and lemon juice and stir. Add to the soup and let it boil up. Take off the heat and add fruit juice. Serve hot. Serves 6.

Rhubarb Soup *(Rabarbrasuppe)*

Cold soup for summertime supper. Serve with zwieback broken into it and more sugar if desired. This soup should be served after the main supper dish.

4 cups young rhubarb, washed and cut into 1/2-inch lengths	6 tablespoons sugar
1 cup water, divided	1/4 teaspoon cinnamon
	1 teaspoon cornstarch

Place rhubarb in saucepan with 1/2 cup water, the sugar, and the cinnamon. Cook covered until tender, about 15 minutes. Mix cornstarch with remaining 1/2 cup water. Remove boiling rhubarb from heat; stir in cornstarch and water mixture. Put back on heat for another boil, then remove and chill. Serves 4.

Apple Soup *(Eplesuppe)*

This soup also is eaten after the main meal. Many drop pieces of zwieback in it.

1-1/2 pounds tart apples
2 quarts cold water
1/4 teaspoon cinnamon
1 slice lemon

1/2 cup sugar or more to taste
1 tablespoon cornstarch dissolved in
1/4 cup water

Peel apples; core and slice. Put into the cold water immediately so they will not darken. Add cinnamon and lemon and cook gently. When tender, stir in sugar, then add cornstarch-water mixture. Bring to boil again. Chill and serve cold. Serves 6.

Split Pea Soup *(Ertesuppe)*

For Henning's Saturday night.

1 cup split peas
1 small ham hock
2 quarts water

2 medium-sized carrots
1/2 small onion
Salt to taste

Wash peas and soak overnight in enough water to cover. In the morning, boil the ham hock in 2 quarts of water for 1/2 hour. Add the peas and soaking water to the ham hock kettle, cover, and boil slowly until the peas are mushy, about 1 hour.

Lift out the ham hock. Scrape and slice carrots, chop onion fine, and add both to the cooked peas. Salt if necessary. Cook for another 30 minutes. If there is meat on the ham hock, chop fine and add to the soup. Serves 6.

Note: *Be sure to have Everyday Pancakes (Almindelige Pannekaker) (page 85) to serve with this on Saturday night, and save the last one for the dog. One of Sigrid's cousins in Norway had a St. Bernard dog, who would sit by the table patiently all through the meal and wait for his pannekakar. When the meal was over, they lifted the cake above his head, he opened his big mouth, the cake went in, he closed his lips, and there was no other movement. It just slid down.*

Sugar strewer from the household of U.V. and Elisabeth Koren, inscribed "E.K."

Vesterheim: Gift of Dr. and Mrs. David Wright, Sr.

Cauliflower Soup *(Blomkålsuppe)*

This is not only delicious, but it also costs almost nothing.

3 tablespoons butter
2 medium-sized carrots, sliced fine
1/4 cup coarsely cut parsley
3 tablespoons flour

1-1/2 quarts cauliflower stock, heated
    (left from other *blomkål* recipes)
1/4 cup half-and-half cream
Salt to taste

In a 2-quart saucepan, melt butter and add carrots and parsley. Cook slowly for 5 minutes, stirring frequently. Sprinkle flour over vegetables and stir well. Add 2 cups heated stock and stir until it makes a smooth sauce. Add the rest of stock and boil until carrots are well done. If there is any cauliflower left from previous meals, cut the stems into fine pieces and add them along with any leftover "flowers." Stir in cream and salt and serve. Serves 6.

Butter Porridge *(Smørgrøt)*

3/4 cup butter
2 cups flour
2 quarts milk

1 teaspoon salt
6 teaspoons butter, approximately
Sugar and cinnamon mixture

Melt butter in a large saucepan. Sift in the flour to make a smooth paste. Boil the milk in another pan and then stir gradually into the butter mixture to make it smooth. Boil 5 minutes. Add salt. Place in individual bowls, make a "butter eye" (a large dab of butter) in the top, and sprinkle with sugar and cinnamon mixture. Serve with a glass of milk. Serves 6.

Rice Porridge *(Risengrynsgrøt)*

This grøt *has been a tradition for Christmas Eve and New Year's Eve for generations. During the holidays, one almond is buried in the* grøt, *and the one who gets it is supposed to be the happiest person during the coming year.*

2 quarts milk
3/4 cup uncooked rice
1/2 teaspoon salt

1-1/2 tablespoons butter, divided
Sugar and cinnamon mixture

If you do not have a big double boiler, make one by placing a pan into a larger pan of water. This porridge takes two hours to cook. Bring milk to a boil; stir in the rice, salt, and 1 tablespoon butter. Cover; stir occasionally so it does not stick. When done, pile into a serving bowl, put a "butter eye" in the middle; pass around along with the sugar and cinnamon. Serves 6.

Cream Porridge (*Rømmegrøt*)

Norway's famous Midsummer Day's treat.

3 cups whipping cream
2 cups flour, divided
8 cups milk, boiling hot

1/2 teaspoon salt
Sugar and cinnamon mixture

In a heavy saucepan, heat the cream for 10 minutes, stirring frequently so that it will not burn. Sift in 1/2 cup flour, beating to make a thin porridge. Let it boil slowly until the butterfat starts to rise. Reduce heat and skim all butter off with a spoon. Put it in a cup to keep warm. Now, gradually sift in the rest of the flour, turning up the heat a little and stirring very well. Add hot milk gradually, stirring all the while. Add salt. *Rømmegrøt* thickens as it stands.

continued

Pile it into a large serving bowl, make a dent in the top, and pour some of the butterfat into it. It will run down the sides of the porridge like lava on Vesuvius. Pass the *rømmegrøt* bowl and the butter cup and let each one help himself. Sprinkle on the cinnamon and sugar mixture and eat! A glass of milk or berry juice is good with this. Serves 6.

Note: *Sigrid contends that you can make* rømmegrøt *from commercial cream, but it does not taste the same as when the cream comes straight from the cow.*

This cast head of an American Indian sits at the base of the handle of the wine decanter pictured on page 55.

Vesterheim Collection

Rømmegrøt the Bridal Porridge

Excerpted from "The Wedding in Norway" by Erna Oleson Xan, who notes that information was provided by Marion Nelson, former director of Vesterheim. He credits, as a reference, Vår Gamie Bondekultur *(Our Old Peasant Culture) by Kristofer Visted and Hilmar Stigum.*

Wedding customs varied slightly from district to district, but certain characteristics seem to have been rather general. The celebration was long. Three days were taken up by rather standard ceremony. The first day was the wedding itself. . . . The ceremonies relating to gifts of money were largely on the second day of the wedding.

The third day was one of eating and general festivity. This is when the bridal porridge was eaten. It consisted of a meal at which the rich sour cream pudding

continued

rømmegrøt was the main dish. It was theoretically prepared by the bride herself, and the master of ceremonies would give a humorous speech about the trials and tribulations that went into the making of the porridge. It was at this meal that the celebrated wedding spoons were used. According to tradition, the bride and groom both ate from these linked utensils as a symbol of unity between them. This practice may not be very old, but it seems to have been well established by the nineteenth century because of the number of examples that exist today.

Wedding spoons hand-carved between 1900 and 1930, probably in the workshop of the Haugen family, Hol, Hallingdal, Norway.

Vesterheim Museum Collection

Fish and Meat

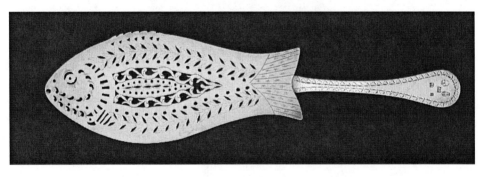

Fish server made in 1792 by Peder Christensen Beyer, Bergen
Vesterheim: Gift of Mr. and Mrs. Storm Bull

VIOLENCE IN THE KITCHEN

She breaks an egg
She beats it up
She whips the cream
She cracks the nuts
She chops the cabbage
She pounds the steak
She punches the dough
She cuts the bread
She scalds the milk
She mashes the potatoes
She shakes the lettuce
She squeezes the lemon
And *slaps* the supper on the table.

—Erna Oleson Xan

Fish and Shrimp in Pastry Shells *(Fiskeboller i Mørdeig)*

A truly Norwegian luncheon served with flatbrød, *tomato wedges, celery pieces, and* Rodgrøt med Fløte *for dessert.*

Pastry shells:
3 cups flour
1 teaspoon baking powder

1/2 teaspoon salt
1-1/4 cups butter
1/2 cup ice water

Filling:
1 can Norwegian fish balls

2 cans small shrimp

White Sauce:
3 tablespoons butter
2 tablespoons flour
1 cup fish stock (add milk to equal 1 cup)

1/4 cup half-and-half cream
1/2 teaspoon salt
Parsley for garnish

33

continued

Pastry shells: Sift flour, baking powder, and salt together into mixing bowl. Cut the butter into it with a pastry blender. Sprinkle ice water over mixture and blend. Chill the dough. To roll out, use a stockinette-covered rolling pin with a canvas-covered board or plastic pastry sheet. Flour both lightly. Roll dough as thin as you can handle it. To shape the shells, lay a saucer on the dough and cut a circle a little bit bigger. Fit this circle on the outside of a 6-ounce ovenproof glass custard cup. Prick top with a fork. Place upside-down on a cookie sheet. Bake at 450° F about 10 minutes. Take out when light brown. Cool, then carefully remove from cup.

Filling: Drain fish balls and save the juice. Cut into 1/2-inch pieces. Drain shrimp.

Sauce: In a saucepan, melt butter; blend in flour until smooth. Gradually add the fish stock, stirring until satin smooth. Add cream and salt, cubed fish balls, and 2/3 of shrimp. Cook slowly, stirring until heated through. When ready to serve, pile fish-shrimp mixture into pastry shells and garnish tops with remaining shrimp and the parsley.

Poached Fish *(Kokt Fisk)*

In Norway, poached fish is traditionally served with melted parsley butter or Hollandaise sauce.

3 pounds frozen fillet of cod or haddock (defrosted)

Tomato wedges for garnish

Melted butter and chopped parsley or Hollandaise Sauce (page 36)

Cut each fillet into individual servings. Drop fillets into a kettle of boiling, salted water. Bring to a boil, reduce heat, and simmer for 10 to 12 minutes. (Hard boiling ruins the fine flavor.) When done, lift fillets out with a slotted spoon. Save the stock to make Hollandaise sauce, if desired. Decorate with tomato wedges. Serves 6.

Hollandaise Sauce *(Hollandsk Saus)*

Although this sauce comes from Holland, it "jumped the border," and has acquired a Norwegian name. This recipe does not curdle.

1 tablespoon flour	4 egg yolks
1/4 teaspoon salt	1/2 cup fish stock
3/4 cup water	2 tablespoons lemon juice
6 tablespoons butter	

Mix flour and salt. Put water in saucepan, stir in flour mixture, and bring to a boil. Take off heat and cool. Partially melt butter and beat into flour mixture, then beat in egg yolks, one at a time. Stir in fish stock. Return to heat and beat until sauce thickens. Remove from heat immediately and stir in the lemon juice.

Fish Soufflé *(Fiskegratin)*

5 tablespoons butter
3 tablespoons flour
2 cups milk
1/2 cup half-and-half cream
1/2 pound cold poached cod or
    haddock (can be leftovers)

4 eggs
1/4 teaspoon salt
1/4 teaspoon grated nutmeg
1/2 cup crushed zwieback or dry
    bread crumbs

Melt butter in a saucepan. Blend in the flour until it makes a smooth paste. Slowly add the milk and cream and stir until smooth. Finely chop the fish and stir into sauce. Beat eggs until light and foamy and fold into fish mixture. Sprinkle in the salt and nutmeg and blend.

37

continued

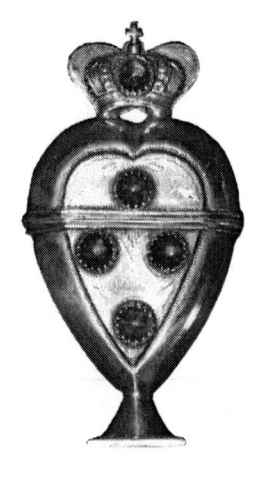

Grease an ovenproof dish. Spoon the soufflé into it and sprinkle zwieback crumbs on top. Bake at 375° F for 45 minutes to 1 hour or until nicely browned on top.

Note: *Norwegians usually serve this with melted butter, but Asparagus Sauce (next recipe) adds a very special taste.*

This perfume bottle features five red stones, called bergkrystall, *or rock crystal, found in the Norwegian mountains.* Vesterheim: Luther College Collection

Asparagus Sauce *(Aspargessaus)*

This is an easy recipe because canned, chopped pieces of asparagus, which you can get in any season and are inexpensive, are just the thing for it.

1 tablespoon butter
1 tablespoon flour
2 cups fish stock

3 tablespoons half-and-half cream
1/2 cup canned asparagus tops and
    stems, drained and chopped

Melt butter in a saucepan. Blend in the flour until smooth. Little by little add the fish stock until all is satin smooth, then stir in the cream. Fold in the asparagus.

Fish Balls and Fish Pudding (*Fiskeboller, Fiskepudding*)

Once a month for years, we (Sigrid and Erna) got together at one of our homes for a Fish Ball dinner. It was our "Sisterhood Ceremony" in honor of our Norwegian heritage and our friendship. A white sauce with capers, shrimp, celery, or lobster is often served with both the fish balls and pudding. —S.G.M.

Fresh fish (haddock is best)	2 cups milk
1 heaping teaspoon potato flour	2 cups cream
Salt to taste	Nutmeg to taste

Work in a cool place to avoid spoiling the fresh fish. Clean the fish and rinse well. Scrape meat from bones and pat dry in a clean cloth. Reserve skin and bones to make fish stock. Then mash fish fine on a board; the scraped fish can also be put through a grinder five times. To a deep soup plate amount of fish, add the potato flour and salt, and stir well for 1/2 hour. Add milk and cream a spoonful at a time until desired consistency is reached; if you are going to make a pudding, the mixture can be a little softer than for fish balls. Season with a little nutmeg.

For Fish Balls, make a stock by boiling the reserved skin and bones in salted water for 10 minutes. Strain. Boil one fish ball to see if it holds together; add a little more potato flour to mixture if needed. Drop teaspoonfuls of the mixture into boiling stock. They will rise to the top when done, about 7 to 8 minutes. These will keep for several weeks if covered in stock and refrigerated.

For Fish Pudding, put the fish mixture into a greased and floured baking dish. Place dish in a pan of boiling water and bake in a 350° F oven for 45 minutes.

Herring Salad *(Sildesalat)*

This makes a beautiful main dish for a buffet supper.

3 salted herring
Chopped, cooked beef or veal to
    equal the amount of herring
2 large potatoes, cooked and cubed
2 medium-sized carrots, grated
1 small onion, finely chopped
1/4 cup chopped sweet pickle
1 cup cream
1 teaspoon vinegar
1 tablespoon sugar

Salt and pepper to taste
For Decoration:
2 eggs, hard-cooked, whites and yolks
    chopped separately
1 cup canned beets (dried on a paper
    towel), chopped fine
1/2 cup grated carrots
1/2 cup sliced, stuffed green olives
Sprigs of parsley

Soak the herring overnight. In the morning, throw soaking water away and cover with fresh water. Boil 10 minutes; drain and cool. Chop herring into small pieces and place in a mixing bowl. Add the chopped beef, potatoes, carrots, onion, and pickle. In another bowl, mix cream, vinegar, sugar, salt, and pepper. Stir well into the herring mixture.

Run cold water into a deep bowl and leave until bowl is chilled, then pour out. Pack the salad into the bowl, chill for several hours, then turn out onto a platter.

Decorate salad in "watermelon stripes," alternating colors—egg whites, beets, egg yolks, then carrots; repeat this order until done. To make divisions between the strips, place a 1/2-inch-wide strip of paper between them while you are working and remove as you go. Decorate the top with sliced olives and parsley.

Boneless Birds *(Benløse Fugle)*

3 pounds flank steak (thick as
    a little finger)
1 teaspoon salt
1/2 teaspoon pepper
1/4 teaspoon ground cloves
Strips (1 x 1") salt pork
    (Raw marrow is better. Finely
    chopped suet will do.)

Flour
2 tablespoons butter
Sauce:
2 tablespoons butter
1-1/2 tablespoons flour
3 cups broth
4 tablespoons sour cream

Pound the flank steak with a meat hammer until it is of even thickness across. Cut into 3- to 4-inch pieces. Mix salt, pepper, and cloves. On each piece of meat, lay a strip of salt pork or 2 teaspoons marrow or suet. Sprinkle with the salt, pepper, and clove mixture. Roll up the meat and tie with cord or heavy white thread. Roll "birds" in flour and brown in the butter. Make the sauce in another pan. Brown the butter slowly, blend in the flour, and add the broth very slowly to make a smooth sauce. Bring to a boil and place the "birds" in it.

Cover tightly and simmer for 1 hour. Add sour cream and simmer a few minutes more. When cooked down, sauce will make the gravy; if necessary, thin with a little water.

Serves 6.

This Norwegian tea strainer was made about 1850.

Vesterheim: Gift of Dr. and Mrs. David T. Nelson

Meat and Soup *(Kjøttsuppe)*

A hearty two-course meal for a cold day.

4-1/2 quarts water
1 large beef soup bone, split in two
1 teaspoon salt
2 pounds beef stew meat
4 carrots, scrubbed and trimmed

2 parsnips, scrubbed and trimmed
2 green onions with tops, cut up
2 stalks celery with leaves, cut up
1/2 cup chopped parsley
5 or 6 boiled potatoes

Place water, beef bone, and salt into large kettle and simmer for 2 hours. Skim off scum as it rises. As water boils away, add more. Remove beef bone and add stew meat to stock. Cook for 1 hour, then add whole carrots, parsnips, and the cut-up onions and celery. Boil slowly for another hour. At the end, there should be 2 quarts of liquid.

This will now make two courses. Lift out the meat and put it into a dish to keep warm. Reserve it for the second course. The first course is soup. Cut up the cooked parsnips and carrots and return them to the soup. Serve with parsley sprinkled on top. The following Dumplings (page 48) make a delicious addition to the soup if you wish to include them. Serve reserved meat with Onion Sauce (page 49) and boiled potatoes as a second course.

Dumplings *(Brødboller)*

A delicious addition to soup.

1 tablespoon butter	2 teaspoons sugar
1 egg	1/4 teaspoon ground cardamom
1 cup milk	Dash of ground cinnamon
1 cup crushed zwieback	

Beat the butter until soft; beat and add the egg. Add milk and stir. Combine remaining ingredients and stir gradually into milk mixture. Dough should be stiff enough to make a ball with a spoon; if not, add a little more crushed zwieback. Dip a teaspoon into water, then into the dough. Immerse into boiling soup and ball will come off. Dumplings will rise to the top when done.

Onion Sauce *(Løksaus)*

4 tablespoons butter, divided
2 tablespoons flour
1 cup hot milk
1/4 teaspoon salt
Dash of pepper

1 medium-sized onion, chopped very
    fine
1/2 cup meat-soup stock
2 tablespoons cream
1/4 teaspoon sugar

Make a white sauce: Over low heat, melt 2 tablespoons butter and blend in flour to make a paste. Add milk gradually, stirring the while, then add salt and pepper.

    Melt 2 tablespoons butter in a saucepan, add onions, and cook until transparent. Slowly blend in the stock and white sauce. Simmer for 15 minutes, then strain mixture through a colander. Reheat and add cream and sugar. Pour sauce over meats. Serves 6 generously.

Pork Tenderloin *(Svinekam)*

An elegant company dinner. When this platter is borne to the table, it reminds the visitor to Norway of the medieval dishes that were "set before the king."

Pork loin, one rib for each person
1 teaspoon salt
1/2 teaspoon pepper
2 cups water
Potatoes and other vegetables
Gravy:
2 tablespoons meat drippings

2 tablespoons flour
1 cup vegetable stock or hot water
Garnishes:
Tomato wedges
Lettuce leaves
Parsley sprigs

tomatoes

Have butcher cut loin just through the bone at each rib for easier cutting and serving. Sprinkle with salt and pepper and place dry in a shallow pan. Bake at 350° F 30 to 35 minutes per pound. When loin begins to brown, add 2 cups water. When the meat begins to recede from the bone, it is well done. Remove the meat to a large platter. Finish cutting through to make individual servings, but keep it together like a whole loin. Place in a warming oven.

To make gravy: In a roasting pan, drain off fat except 2 tablespoons. Heat fat and stir in flour until smooth. Slowly add stock or water and stir until satiny.

While meat is roasting, prepare a variety of vegetables to your taste. Parsleyed potatoes, of course, will be served in a separate dish. Cooked carrots or Brussels sprouts, long green beans, asparagus, cauliflower, peas, or combinations may be arranged artistically around the pork loin, decorating alternately with tomato wedges, lettuce leaves, and sprigs of parsley. Serve gravy in a separate dish.

Mutton and Cabbage *(Får i Kål)*

This is a big dish, and it makes tasty leftovers. In Norway it is said the seventh day is the best. Norwegians use 1-1/2 tablespoons whole black peppercorns, which make a pretty appearance, but which must be fished out as you eat.

1 medium-sized head cabbage	1 teaspoon black pepper
6 pounds mutton breast or leg, or lamb	1/2 cup flour
1-1/2 tablespoons salt	1-1/2 quarts boiling water

Cut cabbage into quarters and remove the core. Cut each quarter crosswise into six pieces. Plunge into salted, boiling water, then place in cold water. Drain.

This is a layered dish. Choose a very large kettle. Cut the raw meat into serving pieces, using the fattest for the bottom layer. Place a third of the meat in kettle. Mix the salt, pepper, and flour. Sprinkle a third of this mixture on the meat, then lay a third of the cabbage. Repeat the layers (meat, flour, cabbage) until all is used.

Pour 1-1/2 quarts boiling water into kettle, cover with tight lid, and bring to a boil. Reduce heat and simmer for 2-1/2 hours. (Stir a couple of times so that top layer goes to bottom.) Add more salt or pepper if necessary. Skim off fat that rises to top.

Serve with boiled parsleyed potatoes.

Meat Cakes *(Kjøttkaker)*

3 pounds stew meat
1/4 pound fresh pork
2 tablespoons cornstarch
1 teaspoon salt
Dash of ground ginger
Dash of nutmeg
1/4 teaspoon pepper

1 cup milk, boiled and cooled
Flour for coating cakes
6 tablespoons butter, divided
2 tablespoons flour
2 cups broth
Salt to taste

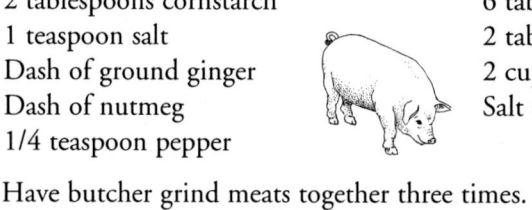

Have butcher grind meats together three times.

Mix cornstarch, salt, and spices and work thoroughly into the meat. Then, little by little, add the cooled milk. Shape the meat into 2-1/2-inch cakes about 1/2 inch

thick. Coat on both sides with a little flour. Melt 2 tablespoons butter in a skillet and brown the cakes, turning carefully. Remove to a bowl.

Melt the remaining 4 tablespoons of butter in the skillet, blend in 2 tablespoons flour, and stir until smooth and brown. Little by little add the broth. Cook, stirring constantly, until smooth and satiny. Add salt to taste. Add the meat cakes and cook for 8 to 10 minutes. Serves 6.

This "Rebecca"-style 1889 wine decanter was made in Oslo by the firm of David Andersen, an innovator in mass-producing high-quality silver and gold objects; the firm is prestigious today. The handle base is pictured on page 28.

Fish in Norway
by Sigrid Marstrander

Since Norway is surrounded by water from north to south and has so many rivers, fjords, and lakes, it is natural that fish is an important part of the menu. When I lived in Norway, it was customary to have four days of fish and three days of meat during the week. One large codfish would make several dinners for the average family, notably fish balls and fish pudding.

The man of the house usually did the fish shopping. In the larger cities there were markets with cement water tanks in which live fish were kept. The man went around inspecting them, and finally pointed to the one he wanted. The merchant hooked it up, and would sometimes kill it for the customer. *Torsk* (cod) was usually carried home to the kitchen alive. Of course, this was in the cities only. I remember once we had a new maid from far out in the country. When it came time to serve the dinner, she was found sitting in the stairway crying. She was afraid of the fish and couldn't kill it!

When Henning and I moved to America, I had a hard time finding the fresh-caught fish he liked so well. As he came in from work, he would say, "I see we're having fish. I smelled it three blocks down the street."

Vegetables

This worn and battered spoon was owned by the Ole Johnson family, and probably was used by the Johnsons to eat mush or stew as they sailed in 1825 on the sloop Restauration, *the first ship that brought Norwegians to the United States.*

Vesterheim: Luther College Collection, Gift of the Ole Johnson family

Mealy Boiled Potatoes *(Kokt Poteter)*

No dinner is complete without this!

1 potato for each person
1/2 teaspoon salt

Parsley, chopped

Peel potatoes very thinly and place in boiling, salted water. When they are done, pour water off. (Save it for soup or gravy, or just drink it. Do not throw away.) Put the pan back on low heat and shake to dry the potatoes, making them very mealy. Turn off the heat; leave potatoes in pan covered with a folded towel across the top. Put lid back on and keep warm until serving time. The towel will absorb the rest of the moisture. At mealtime, sprinkle with chopped parsley.

Greta's Potatoes *(Greta's Poteter)*

8 raw potatoes   Salt to taste

Peel, wash, and dry potatoes. Place them in a greased, shallow pan and bake at 400° F until they are brown and crisp on the outside and done on the inside. When serving, sprinkle with salt. Serve with cold meat and cheese.

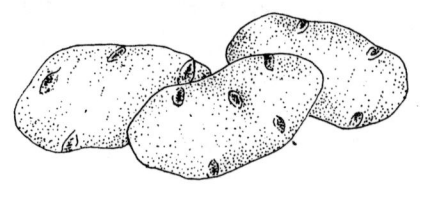

Potato Rolls *(Potetesruletter)*

6 to 8 boiled potatoes, cooled
3 tablespoons melted butter
1 egg yolk
1/2 teaspoon salt
Dash of pepper

2 teaspoons cornstarch
1 egg white
Zwieback or bread crumbs
Deep fat for frying

Put potatoes through a sieve. Add melted butter and egg yolk, salt, and pepper. Sprinkle with cornstarch and mix well. Roll out in finger shapes; dip in slightly beaten egg white, and then in bread crumbs. Place them singly on a large pan or surface to rest for 15 minutes. Then fry in deep fat until light brown. Take up with slotted spoon and drain on paper towel. Serve hot. Serves 6.

Boiled Cauliflower *(Kokt Blomkål)*

1 head cauliflower
2 quarts water
1/2 teaspoon salt

3 tablespoons butter, melted
Parsley, finely chopped

Remove big outer leaves. Cut the stalk off about 1 inch and cut a deep cross on the end to make it cook quicker. Soak cauliflower in cold, salted water for a while to drive out any insects. Boil 2 quarts of water with 1/2 teaspoon salt; put the cauliflower in, head up, and boil for 3 minutes. Take it out of the water; pour cold water over to cool. (This keeps cauliflower white.) Place back into the boiling water, head down this time, and boil for 20 minutes. (Be careful not to cook it to pieces.) Drain and save the water for soup. Serve whole head on a platter; pour melted butter over and sprinkle with parsley. Serves 6.

Cauliflower Soufflé *(Blomkålgratin)*

1 medium-sized cauliflower	4 egg yolks
1/2 cup butter	Salt to taste
1 cup flour	1/8 teaspoon nutmeg
1-2/3 cups hot milk	4 egg whites, stiffly beaten

Boil cauliflower according to previous recipe, but remove from water when not quite done. In another pan, melt butter, add flour, and stir until smooth. Add hot milk slowly and stir until smooth. Cool. Add egg yolks one at a time. Add salt and nutmeg. Fold in stiffly beaten egg whites. Separate cauliflower into flowerettes (not too small) and fold carefully into batter. Spoon into a buttered baking dish and bake at 325° F for about 30 minutes. Serve with the White Sauce used in the following recipe. Serves 6.

Cauliflower with Shrimp *(Blomkål med Reker)*

Served with buttered toast, lettuce, and tomato, this is a favorite ladies' luncheon dish.

1 head cauliflower, cooked according to Boiled Cauliflower recipe (page 62)
1 pound cleaned, fresh, frozen, or canned shrimp
1 teaspoon salt

White Sauce:
2 tablespoons butter
2 tablespoons flour
1 cup hot milk
1/4 teaspoon salt

If using raw shrimp, cook according to directions on package. If canned, drain off liquid. Make a white sauce in double boiler: Melt butter; stir in flour, hot milk, and salt. Cook until thickened, stirring frequently until satiny. Stir in shrimp and heat. Place whole cauliflower on a platter and pour shrimp-in-sauce over it. Serves 6.

Red Cabbage *(Surkål)*

This dish makes a hit wherever it goes. It is good with pork or other meats.

1 large head red cabbage
2 tablespoons butter, divided
1-1/4 teaspoons caraway seeds
1 tablespoon flour

1 teaspoon salt
2 cups meat stock or water
1 tablespoon vinegar
1 tablespoon sugar

Cut away core of cabbage. Soak head in cold, salted water for 10 minutes and drain. Shred into fine strips. Grease bottom of a kettle with 1 tablespoon butter. Layer alternately cabbage, caraway seeds, and dots of butter; sprinkle flour and salt on each layer. Add stock or water. Cover and boil 1-1/2 hours, stirring frequently. Do not let boil dry. Before serving stir in vinegar and sugar. Add more salt if desired. Serves 6.

Glazed Carrots *(Glaserte Gulerøtter)*

6 medium-sized carrots
2 cups boiling water
1 teaspoon salt
4 tablespoons butter

2 teaspoons sugar
1 tablespoon finely
    chopped parsley

Scrape and trim carrots and cut each into four pieces. Place in a saucepan and pour boiling water over them; add salt, butter, and sugar. Cover with a lid and let boil until almost done and water is almost evaporated. Shake the pan so carrots are turned and glazed all over. Sprinkle with chopped parsley. Serves 6.

Carrots with Lemon *(Gulerøtter med Citron)*

1 pound carrots
2 tablespoons butter
2 teaspoons chopped parsley

Juice of half a lemon
Salt and pepper to taste

Wash and scrape carrots. Cut into slices and boil in salted water to cover till tender. Drain and put back over heat to dry, shaking all the while. Add butter, parsley, lemon juice, and a little salt and pepper; stir all together. Serves 6.

Parsnip Balls *(Pastinakboller)*

7 medium-sized parsnips
1 egg yolk, beaten
Salt and pepper to taste
2 tablespoons flour

1 egg white, beaten stiff
1 cup dry bread crumbs
2 tablespoons butter for pan frying or
      fat or vegetable oil for deep-frying

Scrub parsnips and scrape well. Remove stems and tails. Boil in salted water to cover until tender. Drain and dry over heat, shaking constantly. Mash well. Add beaten egg yolk, salt, and pepper, and stir in flour. Cool. Fold in the beaten egg white. Shape into 1-1/2-inch balls. Roll in bread crumbs and either brown in butter in a skillet or deep-fry until golden brown. Serves 6.

Mashed Rutabaga (*Kålrabistappe*)

4 (4-inch) strips salt pork
1 big rutabaga
3 or 4 medium-sized potatoes

1/4 cup margarine
1/2 cup hot milk
Pepper to taste

Boil the salt pork for 1/2 hour in enough water to cover vegetables when added. Remove pork and set aside. Peel rutabaga and potatoes and cut into small pieces. Place rutabaga in the pork water and cook for 1 hour, then add potatoes and cook 20 minutes more. Drain off water. Mash vegetables; add margarine, hot milk, and pepper. Beat until light and fluffy. Keep warm. Fry the salt pork until crisp. When serving, place the heap of mashed vegetables on a platter surrounded by the fried pork. Serves 4.

Onion Soufflé (*Løk Soufflé*)

3 medium-sized onions
2 tablespoons butter
1 tablespoon flour
1/2 cup milk

1/4 teaspoon salt
Dash of paprika
3 egg yolks, slightly beaten
3 egg whites, beaten stiff

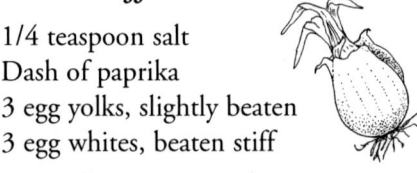

Boil onions until tender and press through a colander. In a saucepan, melt butter, stir in flour to make a paste, and add milk gradually. When smooth and satiny, add onion pulp, salt, and paprika. Bring to a boil and add egg yolks. Remove from heat and fold in the beaten egg whites. Pour soufflé into butter-greased baking dish. Place dish in a shallow pan with hot water. Bake at 350° F for 25 to 30 minutes. Serve immediately. Serves 4.

Sugar Peas in Pods *(Sukkererter)*

1 quart young peas in pods
1 tablespoon butter
2 teaspoons flour

2 teaspoons finely chopped parsley
1/2 teaspoon sugar
1/4 teaspoon salt

Wash pods; remove stems and strings. Cut diagonally into 1-inch lengths. Cover with salted water and boil until tender. When done, drain, and reserve 1 cup of the liquid. In a saucepan, melt butter and stir in the flour to make a paste. Add the pot liquid slowly and bring to a boil. Cook until thickened. Add the chopped parsley, sugar, and salt. Stir sauce into the peas. Serves 6.

Breads and Pancakes

Table setting in the Vidar pattern, silver plate, 1967, Th. Marthinsen Company, Tønsberg. These pieces show the insignia of the Chicago Norske Klub.

Vesterheim: Gift of the Chicago Norske Klub and J. Harry and Josefa Andersen

Christmas Bread *(Julekake)*

1 cup butter
3/4 cup sugar (reserve 2 teaspoons for
    later use)
2 eggs
2 egg yolks
1 teaspoon salt
1/2 teaspoon ground cardamom

1 cup whole milk
2 packages dry yeast
4 cups sifted flour
1 cup seedless raisins
1 cup finely chopped citron
2 egg whites, beaten slightly

In a bowl, cream butter and sugar until light and lemon-colored. Beat the two eggs and egg yolks; add to the butter mixture and stir well. Add salt and cardamom. Heat milk to lukewarm. Pour into a large bowl and sprinkle yeast on it. Add the reserved

continued

2 teaspoons of sugar and stir. When the yeast has bubbled up, add alternately the flour and the butter mixture, beating with a wooden spoon until smooth. Cover and let stand in a warm place until double in bulk. Turn onto a floured board and knead until smooth and elastic. Lastly, knead in the raisins and citron.

If this is going to be one big cake, place the dough into a greased 9-inch tube pan; if two, put into greased loaf pans. Let the dough rise again, covered with waxed paper and a cloth, until double in bulk. Preheat oven to 350° F. Just before placing in oven, brush dough carefully with egg whites to make a glaze. Bake for 50 to 60 minutes.

Rye Bread *(Rugbrød)*

The daily bread of Norway.

1 cup milk
1 package dry yeast
1 teaspoon sugar
4 cups rye flour, divided

1/2 teaspoon salt
2 teaspoons caraway seeds (optional)
1/2 cup lukewarm water

Bring milk to boiling and cool to lukewarm. Pour 1/4 cup into a bowl and sprinkle with the yeast and sugar. Stir in 2 tablespoons of the flour and let bubble and rise for 15 minutes in a warm place. Into another bowl, sift the flour and salt (add caraway seeds if desired). Add the lukewarm water and milk and work to a fine dough. Add the yeast mixture and knead on a floured surface for 15 minutes. Place dough in a

continued

greased bowl and turn dough upside-down. Cover with waxed paper and a towel and let rise in a warm place for 3/4 to 1 hour.

Knead again, using a little more flour, until there are no cracks. Shape into two loaves. Place on a greased baking sheet and let rise again for 15 minutes. Dip a pastry brush in milk and brush tops of loaves. Prick five holes in each loaf to release air bubbles. Bake at 350° F for about an hour.

Note: *Not much wheat is grown in Norway, but rye is grown widely. Rye flour contains very little gluten, so a bread made with all rye flour will be very heavy and dense. Substituting 1 or 2 cups of white flour will result in a lighter loaf.*

Lefse (Rolled-up *Flatbrød*)

3 cups cooked, riced potatoes (cooked
    without salt)
1 tablespoon melted shortening
3/4 cup flour

1 teaspoon sugar
1 teaspoon salt
Butter for spreading
Sugar for sprinkling

Measure riced potatoes into a bowl. Add melted shortening. Sift the flour, sugar, and salt together and add to the potato mixture. Mix well. Form the dough into egg-sized balls. Roll out very thin on a lightly floured pastry cloth using a grooved rolling pin if you have one. Bake on a hot, greased griddle until bubbles form on top. Turn and brown on other side. It should be moist and pliable after it is baked.

continued

Fold each cake in half, then in thirds until it looks like a flat cone. Stack them on a plate and keep a tea towel over them until serving time. Pass the plate at supper so that each person may spread his *lefse* with butter, sprinkle with sugar, or both.

Note: *The traditional* lefse *of Norway is made of mashed potatoes, rye flour, and water. We did not think this would appeal to Americans, so Sigrid got this delightful recipe of Mrs. Clarine Strand of Birmingham, a third-generation Norwegian, who had sent her* lefse *at Christmas time.*

Flatbread *(Flatbrød)*

Welcome at every meal.

2 cups rolled oats
1-1/2 cups whole-wheat flour
1/2 cup white flour
2 tablespoons sugar

1/2 teaspoon salt
1-1/2 cups water
1/2 cup melted butter

Put the dry rolled oats into a blender. Blend, and it will become flour in a few minutes. Sift together with the other flours, sugar, and salt into a bowl; mix in the water and melted butter with a pastry blender to make a nice smooth dough. Chill.

The *flatbrød* will be very thin, so use a pastry cloth or plastic pastry sheet and a stockinette-covered rolling pin. Flour surface and pin slightly. Grease a cookie sheet.

continued

Roll out a piece of dough to fit it. Since you might tear the thin dough while lifting it to the sheet, roll it up on the pin and roll it out onto the cookie sheet. Trim edges.

If you have a *riflet-kjevle,* this is the time to roll it over the dough to make a pattern of holes. If not, prick dough with a fork. Mark the dough into cracker-sized pieces. Bake at 350° F for about 10 minutes. If you put the sheet on the bottom rack first, then shift it to the top rack, it will acquire a nice tan without burning.

Note: *Of course, if you have a big round special griddle as they use in Norway, you may bake it on this, turning the* flatbrød *with two long spatulas. . . . Since it will come off the stove large and round, break into smaller pieces for serving. In Norway, Thorild Andreasdatter Bøe, Erna's grandmother, would have a woman come in to help bake the winter's supply of* flatbrød. *It was then stacked like great phonograph records in the rat-proof* stabbur, *the food building.*

White Bread *(Loff)*

This is a special bread for Sunday morning to eat with eggs. For other meals, it is often buttered and served with soup.

2-1/2 cups milk, divided

2 packages dry yeast

1 tablespoon sugar

4 cups white flour, divided

2 cups rye flour

1 teaspoon salt

Bring milk to a boil and cool to lukewarm. Place 1/2 cup of lukewarm milk into a big bowl; stir in the yeast, sugar, and 1 tablespoon white flour. Let it bubble and rise in a warm place for 15 minutes. Sift the white and rye flours together, add the salt, and stir into remaining 2 cups of lukewarm milk. Work to a fine dough, then add the yeast mixture and stir well. Turn onto a floured board and knead for 15 minutes.

81

continued

White Bread *continued*

Grease and flour two loaf pans. Shape the dough into two pretty loaves, place them into the pans, and let rise for 1 hour in a warm place. Preheat oven to 350° F and bake for about 1 hour.

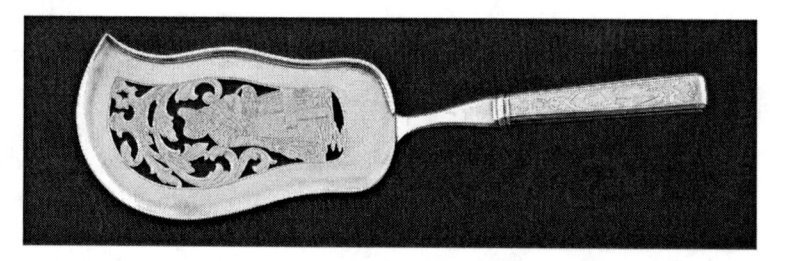

Fish server with a scene of a woman and a basket of fish.
Vesterheim: Gift of Mr. and Mrs. Storm Bull

Potato Cakes *(Poteteskake)*

If you go to a kaffistova *(coffee house) in the afternoon in Norway, you will get* poteteskake, vaffler, *or* lefse.

1 cup white flour	1/2 teaspoon salt
1 cup rye flour	2 cups mashed potatoes, cooled

Sift the flours and salt together and mix with the mashed potatoes to a smooth dough. Roll out saucer-sized cakes, knife thin. (If they are thick in the middle and lumpy, they will not cook evenly.) Put griddle on slow heat and grease. Cook cakes until brown on bottom; turn and brown other side. Serve with butter, sugar, honey, Norwegian goat cheese, or a mild Cheddar cheese.

Sour Cream Waffles *(Vaffler)*

2 cups sour cream
2 eggs
1 cup flour
1 teaspoon baking powder
1/2 teaspoon baking soda

1/2 teaspoon salt
2 tablespoons sugar
1/2 teaspoon ground cardamom
2 tablespoons water

Beat sour cream until fluffy. In a separate bowl, beat the eggs until light. Combine with cream and beat again. Sift together the dry ingredients and fold gently into the sour cream and egg mixture. Add the water. Grease a medium-hot waffle iron and bake the waffles until golden brown. If you must wait to serve them, put them on a rack in the oven to keep warm. Makes about 12.

Everyday Pancakes *(Almindelige Pannekaker)*

Pea (page 22) or vegetable soup followed by these pancakes was a favorite Saturday night menu for Sigrid and Henning. "Tjafs" (their little terrier named after a Norwegian comic strip dog) would get the last pancake.

4 eggs
1 quart milk (or buttermilk)
4 cups flour

1/2 teaspoon salt
Margarine for frying

Beat eggs well. Add milk and flour alternately. (If buttermilk is used, add 1/2 teaspoon baking soda to flour.) Add salt; stir until smooth. Melt margarine in skillet, spoon batter in, and cook until cakes are firm enough to turn. Flip over and brown on other side. Keep warm in a large, covered bowl. Serves 6.

Hearty Pork Pancakes *(Fleskepannekaker)*

For the working man. Believe it or not, Sigrid insists that Norwegians eat a buttered slice of bread with this for supper, and nothing else except a cup of hot coffee.

4 to 6 strips salt pork (streak of fat, streak of lean)

Batter from Everyday Pancakes (page 85)
2 tablespoons chopped chives

Cut rind off pork; place in boiling water in a large skillet. Boil 3 minutes to extract the salt. Pour off water. Fry pork in the skillet until light brown. Pour off most of the grease. Arrange pork in skillet in serving sections. Cover all carefully with pancake batter. Sprinkle with chives and cook over low heat until it is firm all the way through. Does not have to be turned. To serve, cut into individual pieces.

Finer Pancakes (*Finere Pannekaker*)

For dessert.

6 eggs
1 cup half-and-half cream
4 tablespoons flour
1 cup milk

1/2 teaspoon salt
1 teaspoon sugar
Margarine for frying
Sugar and/or jam

Beat eggs until they foam. Add the cream and stir in the flour until smooth. Add milk, salt, and sugar. Let stand for 2 hours "so the flour can expand," as they say in Norway. Use an 8-inch skillet. Pancakes are much easier to handle in a small skillet. Grease skillet with margarine before making each pancake. Put just enough batter in

continued

to cover bottom of skillet. Pancakes must be thin. Cook over very low heat. When they are firm enough, turn; cook other side until light brown. Keep warm in a covered bowl until dessert time. Serve with sugar and/or jam. Makes about 16.

This 1699 silver tankard has a hammered body with deep repoussé and chased floral decoration above each of the three claw and ball feet.

Vesterheim: Gift of Martha Hodgin

Cakes, Cookies, and Desserts

Coffee pot from the family of Cristian Lange, winner of the Nobel Peace Prize in 1921. It is similar to pieces made by several distinguished goldsmiths working in Christiania/Oslo in the late nineteenth century.

Vesterheim Museum Purchase

Baking for Weddings

Excerpted from an article by Erna Oleson Xan as told to her by Thurine Oleson, originally printed in Wisconsin My Home.

By the time I was seventeen, I was a pretty good baker and cook, and had the honor of being asked to bake at two weddings. . . . I baked quite a few cakes . . . light ones and dark ones.

    . . . It took us two or three days to bake enough cakes for this affair (a large wedding). Another girl helped me, but said she would not take the blame if things went wrong, so it was up to me to go ahead. Oh, of all the cakes at this wedding! I guess they expected seventy or eighty people. We made white cakes, dark cakes, silver and gold cakes, chocolate, and coconut cakes, maybe a couple of each kind.

Layers and loaf cakes, too. The wedding cake was a three-tiered fruit cake, filled with all kinds of raisins and currants and maybe citron. The bottom was made in a good-sized round milk pan, the next a little smaller pan, and the top the smallest of all. It was a pretty white-frosted cake, and good tasting. We had everything we wanted to do with, plenty of eggs, cream, butter and milk in those days, for you could not get much for anything at the store, so we did not have to spare the ingredients. Then there was lovely bread and those good sweet raised biscuits with currants, shortening and sugar in them. . . . Luckily, I was not responsible for all this food, just the cakes and cookies. And don't think any of us got paid for it. It was supposed to be a great honor, and it was. You had to have people you could trust and who knew their business when you had such an important event as a wedding.

Duchess Cake *(Hertuginnekake)*

This is Sigrid's birthday cake.

6 large eggs
1 cup sifted sugar
1-1/2 cups sifted flour
1/2 teaspoon baking powder
Filling:
2 cups whipping cream
2 tablespoons sugar
1 cup finely chopped blanched almonds

1/2 teaspoon vanilla
Glaze:
1 cup confectioner's sugar
2 tablespoons cold water
1/2 teaspoon lemon juice
Decoration:
1 cup stiffly whipped cream or
   1 carton Cool Whip®

Let your mixer do the work! Beat eggs in large bowl until light and lemon-colored. Gradually add the sugar and let the mixer work at medium speed for 30 minutes. Sift flour and baking powder together. Remove bowl from mixer and begin sifting flour mixture over egg mixture, gently folding over with a spoon until all flour is incorporated.

Grease bottom of a tube pan, then cut a circle of waxed paper to fit the bottom. Grease the paper and place on bottom of pan. Dust the whole pan with flour. Carefully spoon in the batter and smooth the top to make level. Bake at 325° F for 50 minutes. Cake should shrink slightly away from sides of pan when done. Invert pan to cool, then remove cake to a cake rack.

Prepare filling: Whip cream stiffly, add sugar, and fold in almonds and vanilla.

continued

Assemble cake: Cut into three even layers, using toothpicks as guides. Place bottom layer on a cake plate and cover with half the filling. Put second layer on and use remainder of filling. Place top layer on and glaze the cake. When glazing is dry, place cake in refrigerator for a while, then decorate the cake in a fancy way.

Prepare glaze: Mix all ingredients together well and spread on top of cake with knife or spatula that is dipped repeatedly in warm water.

Decorate: Fill decorator tube half full with whipped cream. Use a fancy tip to make a wreath around the cake. Put pretty little mounds in the middle. In summer, decorate with fresh raspberries or strawberries; in winter, crystallized fruit. You can let your imagination run wild, but it all spells "Happy Birthday!" to your own "Duchess" or "Duke."

Prince's Cake *(Fyrstekake)*

This is a cake fit for a prince, but nobody knows which prince, so in 1974, Ingrid and Erna dedicated theirs to Norway's then-newest infant Prince Haakon Magnus, son of Crown Prince Harald and Crown Princess Sonja.

1 cup flour
1/2 cup sugar
1 teaspoon baking powder
1/2 cup butter
1 egg
1 teaspoon almond extract

Filling:
1/2 cup unblanched almonds
2/3 cup confectioner's sugar
1/4 teaspoon cinnamon
1/4 teaspoon ground cardamom
3 tablespoons water
1 egg white

continued

Sift flour, sugar, and baking powder together and add to butter as for making pastry. Add whole egg and almond extract and knead well. Cut the dough into two pieces. One part is rolled out to a 1/4-inch-thick round. Place on a greased baking sheet.

To prepare filling, leave skin on almonds. Wipe them clean between wet cloths. Grind once in a meat grinder or food processor until they look like small grains. Sift confectioner's sugar with spices and add to the almonds. Add water and stir to a heavy paste.

Spread filling over rolled-out round of dough to within 1/4 inch of edge. Roll out the other half of dough to "half the thickness of little finger" (about 1/4 inch). Cut into strips 1/2 inch wide. (These are pretty if cut with pink-edged cutter.) Weave strips in and out like lattice-work over the filling. Leftover pieces are made into a 3/4-inch-thick ring that goes all the way around the edge of cake. Beat egg white slightly and brush on pastry on top of cake. Bake at 350° F for 25 minutes. Serves 6.

Potato Torte *(Fin Potetkake)*

For coffee time or teas.

1/2 cup hot mashed potatoes
5 tablespoons butter
1/2 cup sugar
1 cup uncooked rolled oats
12 drops almond extract

Glaze *(Flormelis Glasur)*:
2 cups confectioner's sugar
3 tablespoons boiling water
1 teaspoon vanilla

Put potatoes into a mixing bowl; add in succession the butter, sugar, oats, and almond extract. Stir until well mixed. On a greased cookie sheet spread the dough to the size and shape of a dinner plate. Bake at 325° F until light brown. Remove from oven and cool, then glaze. **For glaze:** Mix all ingredients till smooth and easy to spread. Makes about 12 pieces.

Cream Puff Pretzel *(Vandbakkelskringle)*

1 cup water	**Icing:**
1/2 cup butter	1-1/2 cups confectioner's sugar
1 cup flour	Water (just a little) to make a paste
4 eggs	1 teaspoon vanilla

Boil water and butter in a saucepan until butter is melted. Remove from heat and add flour all at once. Stir quickly; put back on heat and stir until it forms a ball. Beat in eggs one at a time. Remove from heat and cool slightly.

Preheat oven to exactly 425° F. Grease baking sheet and spoon mixture by tablespoons to make shape of a big pretzel. Bake for 20 minutes. Reduce heat to 325° F

and bake for 15 minutes more. At the end of this time, pinch pretzel gently to see if it is firm. If not, let it bake another 5 minutes. Don't over bake. Cool on the tin.

Icing: Mix ingredients together and drizzle over the pretzel, then remove pretzel to a serving plate. Each serving gets about 1 tablespoon icing. Serves about 14.

This is one of fifty silver snuffboxes commissioned by Crown Prince Karl Johan to give to people who did some special service. It was made in 1836.
Vesterheim: Gift of Bruce Hitman

Christmas in Norway

Excerpted from an article by Erna Oleson Xan as told to her by Sigrid Marstander.

The crowning holiday of the year was Christmas. A month ahead, *Tante* Ida, with whom I lived, started housecleaning. . . .

After the cleaning was over, the baking started. Cookies enough to last through Easter were made at this season, for they were all so rich that they improved by ripening. For these cookies, fine Hungarian flour was used, and day by day, hundreds of cookies were stored in tin boxes. This was one activity in which all women of the house took part, and even *Tante* Ida came out to the kitchen to help.

I beat the twelve eggs for *fattigmann* (poor man's cookies, a joke), and mixed the flour and sugar. They were rolled out and cut leaf-thin with a *trinse,* a roller with a wavy edge. Then I slit a hole in the middle of each one and turned one of the points through the slit. Anna P. had to fry them in lard, however, for it was dangerous for a young girl who might get splattered with the hot fat.

There were *Berlinerkranser* (Berlin wreaths), *smørkranser* (butter rings), *sandkaker* (sand cakes), following each other in fragrant succession. One older lady apologized that she had only eighteen kinds of cookies for Christmas.

When this job was out of the way, Anna P. had to turn her hand to the special meats that were prepared each year. . . . On Christmas Eve Day, fresh bread was made from white flour, butter, sugar, egg, yeast, and lots of currants. This was a great treat, for during the year rye bread was eaten, and the whole-grain flatbread made out in the country in large round sheets. None of this good food could be touched until Christmas Eve, which was the highlight of the entire holiday.

continued

. . . Everybody loved everybody at Christmas, and everybody had to have a good time. . . . The first course was always fish pudding, the second was reindeer with cream gravy. . . . Reindeer tasted like venison, but with a wilder flavor. Sometimes there was half a ptarmigan for each person instead. It also had a wild taste. This course was served with boiled potatoes, peeled, cooked and dried until mealy. There were always imported vegetables—Brussels sprouts or *petit pois* from France, and native cabbage and carrots. It would not be complete without the country *flatbrød*.

For dessert a light pudding, perhaps made of rice with chopped almonds, sugar, gelatin, and topped with whipped cream. It was called rice cream, and was often served with a red fruit sauce, such as strawberry juice thickened with cornstarch.

When the meal was over, the children could think of nothing but the tree in the closed parlor. . . . But the end of the meal was not yet, for the after-dinner coffee was not yet served, and to omit it would be unthinkable.

After that, *Tante* Ida and Uncle Evenson got up, and with great deliberation that made the children "crazy," went into the parlor and shut the doors behind them. This was so no one would see them lighting the dozens of twisted red candles on the tree.

When they flung open the doors, there in the middle of the room was the tall green Norwegian spruce reaching to the ceiling with candles ablaze and little Norwegian flags gleaming in the candlelight. With pride I looked at the little heart-shaped baskets I had made and filled with nuts and raisins. Real, little Norwegian apples swung and twisted on the branches. Colored-paper chains were looped about the tree. On the top was a big star, and little angels were on the branches.

Before the presents under the tree could be distributed, Uncle Evenson got down the Bible and read the Christmas story again. Then the family joined hands and

continued

circled the tree again and again, singing. The last song was always:

"You green and glittering tree, Good Day!
How welcome you are to us today
With your Norwegian flags, and candles alight
And high in the top the star so bright,
Yes, the star must shine thus
For it must remind us
Of the Savior Child that is born tonight."

. . . The family burst into song all during the evening. Nuts were cracked. Apples and dried fruit were munched. Presently Uncle Evenson said his watch was tired and wanted to go to bed in its new little pillow. So we all trooped to bed, because all had to be up and dressed and at the cathedral by seven the next morning.

Cream Patches (*Fløtelapper*)

These should be about the shape of patches on a pair of pants; this is where they get the name.

3 eggs, beaten
1 pint half-and-half cream
5 tablespoons flour
1 tablespoon sugar

1/4 teaspoon salt
1/4 teaspoon ground cardamom
Margarine for frying
Sugar, syrup, or jam for topping

Beat the eggs until foamy. Add half-and-half alternately with the flour and beat until smooth. Then add sugar, salt, and cardamom. Melt margarine in a large skillet. Drop dough by tablespoonfuls and cook until firm; turn and cook till light brown. At the table, top them with sugar, syrup, or jam. Serves 6.

"World's Best" Syrup Cookies *(Sirupskaker– "Verdens Beste")*

In Sigrid's childhood, syrup came in little kegs with a spigot. One went to the Kolonial Butikk (grocery) with one's own bucket or pitcher and bought as much as it would hold.

1 cup margarine
1 cup sugar
1/2 cup light corn syrup
2 tablespoons water

4 cups flour
1/2 teaspoon baking soda
2 teaspoons cinnamon
1/2 teaspoon ground cloves

In a small saucepan, heat the margarine, sugar, and syrup. After it is warmed, add the

water. Cool. Sift flour, baking soda, and spices together and stir into the syrup mixture. Shape the dough into two long rolls about 2 inches in diameter. Wrap each roll in waxed paper and store in refrigerator overnight.

The next day, remove waxed paper and cut roll into thin slices and place on greased cookie sheet. Bake at 375° F about 10 minutes or until done. Makes over 100 cookies.

This tomling, *or brandy cup, is of the late baroque style. It was probably made around 1700.*
Vesterheim: Luther College Collection

Cornucopias *(Kremmerhus)*

Teflon® and Cool Whip® may not have been found in the early Norwegian kitchen, but they are convenient substitutes for an iron griddle and whipped cream.

3/4 cup plus 2 tablespoons butter	6 egg whites
3/4 cup sugar	**Filling:**
1-3/4 cups flour	Cool Whip or other whipped topping
1 teaspoon vanilla	Strawberry jam

Cream butter and sugar until light and lemon-colored. Stir in the flour and vanilla. Beat egg whites until very stiff. Fold egg whites gently into the butter mixture. Grease a Teflon (nonstick) baking sheet and drop the dough by teaspoonfuls onto sheet. With a long knife or spatula, flatten each to thin rounds of even thickness all the way across. (If edges are too thin or middle too thick, they will crack when rolled.) Bake at 300° F until light tan, about 10 minutes.

Open the oven but do not take sheet of cookies out of oven. Remove one cookie at a time with a spatula, and quickly roll over a wooden-spoon handle, or better, a cone-shaped wooden *Kremmerhus*-form (if you have one). If the cookie gets brittle, put it back into the oven for a few minutes, then roll again. These stiffen almost instantly out of the oven. Makes about 60.

Just before serving, mix Cool Whip and strawberry jam and stuff some into each cornucopia. You will have instant fame as a gourmet cook!

Butter Rings *(Smørkranser)*

This is a good standby cookie the year around.

2 eggs
1 cup sugar
2 tablespoons finely chopped
   blanched almonds

1 teaspoon vanilla
4 cups flour
1-1/2 cups butter or margarine

Beat eggs and sugar until light and lemon-colored. Add chopped almonds and vanilla. With hands, add flour and butter alternately until dough is smooth. Put into a cookie press with small star-shaped opening. Press out a long length and then cut into 4-inch pieces. Turn each piece into a circle. Place on a greased cookie sheet and bake at 375° F for 10 to 12 minutes or until light tan. Makes about 120.

Oatmeal Macaroons *(Havremakroner)*

Everybody asks for this recipe. It is easy, cheap, and delicious.

1 cup melted butter or margarine	1/2 teaspoon almond extract
1 cup sugar	1 cup flour
1 egg, beaten	1 teaspoon baking powder
4 tablespoons cream	2-1/2 cups rolled oats

Mix butter and sugar until fluffy. Add beaten egg, then the cream and almond extract. Beat well. Sift flour and baking powder. Add this to the butter mixture and beat again. Stir in the oats and mix well. Place by teaspoonfuls on a greased baking sheet. Bake at 250° F for 20 minutes or until dry and crisp. Makes about 75.

Berlin Wreaths (Berlinerkranser)

Almost everybody in Norway makes these cookies for Christmas. They melt in the mouth. Jon Rolf Marstrander, Sigrid's grandson, called these favorite cookies "The Crossovers."

4 hard-cooked egg yolks, cooled
4 raw egg yolks
1 cup plus 2 tablespoons sugar
4 cups flour
2-1/4 cups sweet butter

Topping:
4 slightly beaten egg whites
1/2 pound sugar lumps, coarsely
    crushed

Mash the four hard-cooked egg yolks and mix with the four raw yolks until smooth.

Add the sugar and beat well. Alternately add the flour and butter and knead until smooth. Chill for 1 hour.

To make cookies, pinch off a lump of dough and roll into pencil shapes on a lightly floured canvas-covered board to a thickness of a little finger. Cut into 5-inch lengths. Cross ends over to make a wreath. Dip cookies into egg white and sprinkle with coarsely crushed sugar. Lay on a greased cookie sheet and bake at 375° F until lightly tan, about 10 to 12 minutes. Makes about 125.

Stacked Cookies *(Bordstabelbakkels)*

2 eggs
2 tablespoons cream
1 cup sugar
4 cups flour, sifted
2 cups sweet butter or margarine,
    melted

Icing:
3 egg whites
1 cup confectioner's sugar
1 cup chopped blanched hazelnuts

Beat eggs, cream, and sugar until light and lemon-colored. Add flour and butter alternately. Chill. Roll very thin and cut into long strips 1 inch wide. Bake on a greased cookie sheet at 350° F until very light tan. Check at 10 minutes. Take from oven and cut into 4-inch lengths while still warm. Cool.

Prepare icing: Beat egg whites to stiff peaks. Add confectioner's sugar gradually, then fold in the nuts. In the middle of each cookie, lay a strip of frosting decoration. Put cookies back into a 200° F oven and dry the frosting. Remove when dry.

Note: *To serve, lay a paper doily on a plate and stack the cookies like lumber into a three-cornered hollow tower. Makes a very pretty centerpiece for the table.*

This straight-sided beaker was brought to the United States by a Norwegian newspaper reporter covering the Chicago World's Fair in 1893.
Vesterheim: Gift of Margit McManus

115

Children's Cookies *(Pleskener)*

2 eggs
2 egg yolks
1 cup sugar
1-1/2 cups flour

3/4 cup cornstarch
1 teaspoon vanilla
Candied citron, finely chopped

Beat eggs, yolks, and sugar until light and lemon-colored. Sift together flour and cornstarch and stir into the egg mixture. Add vanilla. Grease a cookie sheet and drop the dough by teaspoonfuls. Place a little citron in the middle of each. Bake at 325° F until light tan. Makes about 75.

Sand Cakes *(Sandkaker)*

A luncheon dessert in tartlet cups.

1 cup butter or margarine	**Filling:**
1 cup confectioner's sugar	1 pint whipping cream
1 egg	1 tablespoon sugar
2 cups sifted flour	1/4 teaspoon almond extract
1/4 cup blanched ground almonds	Strawberry or raspberry jam for decoration

Cream butter; add sugar and stir until lemon-colored. Add egg and beat well. Add sifted flour and ground almonds. Butter tartlet tins (small round tins with ruffled

continued

edges) and press dough to inside, just to the rim. Bake at 350° F for about 12 minutes or until light golden brown. Cool slightly and invert to remove pastry cups from tins.

Filling: Combine first three ingredients and beat until stiff. Do not fill until just before serving or they will become soggy. At dessert time, fill tartlet cups with whipped cream mixture and place a teaspoonful of red jam on top. Makes about 60.

Peasant Girls with Veils *(Tilslørtebondepiker)*

Nobody could tell just where this dish got its fancy name, but it appears as this in 100-year-old cookbooks. When it is served, though, in a sparkling cut-glass bowl adorned with whipped cream and ladled out with a sterling silver spoon, it really is "all dressed up."

1/4 cup butter
2 cups finely crushed zwieback
1 tablespoon sugar

1/2 teaspoon cinnamon
1 cup jam or applesauce
1 cup whipped cream, sweetened

Melt butter in skillet over low heat. Add zwieback mixed with sugar and cinnamon and stir until light brown. Cool. In a dessert bowl, alternate three layers of zwieback mixture and two layers of jam or applesauce and cream. Top with whipped cream. Serves 4 to 5.

Prune Compote *(Sviskekompot)*

12 ounces pitted dried prunes
1 cup prune juice
1 tablespoon sugar
1/4 cup apple or orange juice

2 tablespoons cornstarch
1/3 cup water
Whipped cream with sugar and
    vanilla to taste

Wash prunes. Soak them overnight in about a quart of water. Next morning, boil in a covered kettle for about 1/2 hour. Take them up with a slotted spoon and save the juice. Cool, then place in a serving dish. Strain the juice and put one cupful into a small saucepan. Add sugar and apple or orange juice. Bring to a boil. Stir cornstarch into the 1/3 cup water and add to juice in the pan. Bring to a boil again, stirring constantly. Take off the heat and cool slightly. Pour over the prunes and serve with whipped cream on top.

Apricot Compote *(Aprikoskompot)*

12 ounces dried apricots
2 tablespoons sugar

Sweetened whipped cream or
half-and-half cream

Wash apricots. Soak in water to cover overnight. Next morning, add sugar and cook slowly until they are mushy. Cool and spoon into individual dishes. Serve with sweetened whipped cream or half-and-half.

Eggedosis *(Eggedosis)*

This is a traditional treat on May 17, Norway's "Fourth of July." It's rich and delicious. You'll remember the taste forever. Any number can be served if you use 1 egg yolk and 2 teaspoons sugar per person. Serve with dainty cookies.

5 egg yolks
10 teaspoons sugar

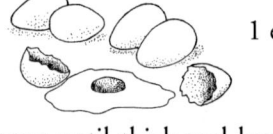

1 egg white, stiffly beaten

Beat egg yolks and sugar until thick and lemon-colored. Fold in stiffly beaten egg white. Serve in punch cups and eat with a spoon. Serves 5.

Note: *Please be aware of the caution regarding consumption of raw eggs.*

Red Berry Pudding with Cream *(Rødgrøt med Fløte)*

This is Norway's national dessert. It can be made also with fresh currants or blackberries, or canned wild blueberries or blackberries.

1 (10-ounce) box frozen strawberries
1 (10-ounce) box frozen raspberries
Water equal to berries and juice

5 tablespoons cornstarch
5 tablespoons sugar
Whipped cream, Cool Whip®,
   or half-and-half

Place berries and water in a saucepan and cook for 5 minutes. Strain through a sieve. This should make about 4-1/2 cups juice. Mix the cornstarch and sugar with a little

continued

water to make a thin paste. Bring the juice to a boil again. Take off heat and stir in the cornstarch mixture. Bring back to a boil quickly, and after 2 minutes, take it off the stove. Cool a little before pouring into a glass bowl or individual serving dishes. (Don't crack the dishes!) To prevent skin from forming, sprinkle a little sugar on top.

Rødgrøt is better if made several hours ahead or the day before serving. At dessert time, top with whipped cream, Cool Whip, or half-and-half cream.

Rice Cream (*Riskrem*)

This is best if made a day ahead.

2-1/4 cups milk
1/4 cup rice
1-1/2 tablespoons sugar
4 tablespoons blanched and
    chopped almonds
2 tablespoons butter
1 pint whipping cream, whipped stiff

1 teaspoon vanilla
1 envelope unflavored gelatin
1/2 cup cold water
Red Sauce:
1 box frozen strawberries
1 cup water
1-1/2 tablespoons cornstarch

Put milk in top of a double boiler and bring to a boil. When it is bubbling around the edge, add the rice and stir. Let cook for about 50 minutes or until rice is well

continued

done. While still hot, add sugar, almonds, and butter. Let cool completely, then fold in the stiffly beaten cream and the vanilla.

Sprinkle gelatin over cold water in a small saucepan. Place over low heat, stirring constantly until gelatin dissolves (about 3 minutes). Cool. Fold into the rice and whipped cream mixture. Spoon into a big, pretty bowl and refrigerate.

Prepare red sauce: Boil strawberries and water for 5 minutes. Dissolve cornstarch in a little water and stir into the sauce; bring to a boil, stirring constantly. Remove from heat and cool. When serving, pass the bowl of rice cream around the table followed by a pitcher of the red sauce to pour over the rice. Serves 8.

Caramel Pudding (*Karamelpudding*)

This dish is best if made as much as a day ahead of time and kept chilled.

Glaze:
1-1/4 cups granulated sugar
1-1/2 cups water
Custard:
5 egg yolks

3 egg whites
3 tablespoons sugar
1 pint half-and-half cream
1/2 cup milk
1 teaspoon vanilla

Put sugar and water in an iron or other heavy skillet. Boil until it gets dry and starts to melt and become golden brown. Pour this immediately into a dry round or oblong mold and turn mold around quickly until glaze covers the sides and bottom of mold entirely. Keep turning until glaze stiffens.

continued

Preheat oven to 325° F. Beat the five egg yolks, three egg whites, and the sugar until light and lemon-colored. In a small saucepan, bring cream and milk to a boil; remove from heat and add vanilla. Pour it slowly over the egg mixture, beating constantly. Cool completely and pour it into the mold. Now, place the mold into a pan with water halfway up the sides. Put in preheated oven and bake for 1-1/2 hours. The water in the pan must be kept at the boiling point all the time. If it evaporates, add more boiling water. Take pudding out of the oven and water-bath and let cool. When cooled, invert the custard on a serving plate with an edge to keep the glaze from running off. Serves 4 or 5.

Apple Pie

As American as "Mom." My "Mom" was born on December 27, 1866, at Winchester, Wisconsin, six months after her parents arrived in America. She was their first American.—E.O.X.

Pastry for Double Crust:
1/2 cup corn oil
1/4 cup cold milk
2 cups sifted flour
1 teaspoon salt
Filling:
3/4 cup sugar
1/4 cup flour

Dash of salt
1/4 teaspoon nutmeg
1/4 teaspoon cinnamon
6 or 7 cups peeled, cored, and sliced tart, juicy apples
2 tablespoons butter

129

continued

Combine the corn oil and milk together in a measuring cup. Mix flour and salt in a bowl. Dig a little hole and dump oil and milk into it. Stir lightly with a fork until well-blended and dough "cleans" the sides of the bowl. Press into a smooth ball and divide, making one part bigger.

Tear off four 12-inch squares of waxed paper. Wipe surface top with damp cloth to keep waxed paper from slipping. Place smaller ball between two papers, and, with a rolling pin, roll dough into a 12-inch circle. Discard top paper. Lift bottom paper and crust and lay upside-down in pie pan. While peeling paper away, pat crust into place, leaving no bubbles. Handle dough as little as possible. Trim edges a little bigger than rim of pan.

Roll out upper crust in the same way. Remove top paper. With a knife tip, cut a leaf design in it like Mom used to do (see illustration, next page).

Let top crust remain on the paper while you prepare the filling.

Filling: Combine sugar, flour, salt, and spices; sprinkle over the apples and stir gently. Heap into bottom crust. Dot with butter. Lift waxed paper and top crust and flop crust over the apples. Discard paper. Trim crust about 1/4 inch bigger than bottom crust and tuck extra dough under rim of bottom crust. Press rim all around with tines of a fork or flute with your fingers. This will keep the juice from running over. Bake at 450° F for 10 minutes. Turn down heat to 350° F for 35 to 40 minutes more until crust is golden brown and juice is bubbling through the design.

Doilies at Vesterheim

Norwegian thrift is expressed in this Norwegian tray cover: "Crumbs are also bread." Marion Nelson, former Vesterheim director, recalled that in his student days in Oslo his hostess would ritualistically collect the crumbs from the table and place them in a box on the windowsill saying, "Fuglen og de fattige må også have sit." (Birds and the poor must also get their share.)

"Giv os Idag vort daglige Brød."
(Give us this day our daily bread.)

This breakfast doily in satin stitch has the simple message "Spis godt stegt brød," *translated as* "Eat well toasted bread."

A mother cooking porridge finds that she is getting an extra draft on the fire from a nisse *(elf). The inscription* "Hjelp i huset" *means "Help in the house."*

135

Tray doily in satin and chain stitch embroidery has the inscription
"Kaffe gi'r Humør" *(Coffee makes the spirits bright.)*

VESTERHEIM: A Home in the West

Visitors to the picturesque northeast Iowa community of Decorah cross the threshold of Vesterheim's Norwegian-American Museum and enter a world of nautical daring, prairie plunder, and deep-seated faith, reliving the saga of the Norwegian immigrant life in America, their *vesterheim,* their western home. With sixteen historic buildings in the main complex and two National Register sites just outside the city, Vesterheim is the largest and most comprehensive museum in the United States dedicated to a single immigrant group. Today, Vesterheim houses more than 24,000 artifacts, including important collections of fine, decorative, textile, and folk arts.

    Decorah has attracted Norwegian settlers since the 1850s. The Vesterheim

continued

beginnings, created in 1877 by Luther College, established the first immigrant ethnic museum in America, followed in 1913 by a pioneering effort in conceiving one of the country's earliest outdoor historical museum complexes.

Today, the independent, nonprofit museum continues to recognize the exceptional achievements of Norwegian Americans in venerating and preserving their material culture. The museum's permanent collection is organized on a grand scale around the immigrant theme: from life in Norway, through the Atlantic crossing, to life in America, with complete Norwegian and pioneer houses and interiors, and a breathtaking ship gallery three stories high. Visitors witness the entire history of a proud, courageous people in the beauty of Norwegian textiles and traditional dress; in the lovely, sometimes fantastical painting called rosemaling (rose painting); in the Spartan furniture and housewares of early pioneer life; and in the impressive fine art that Norwegian-American culture eventually fostered.

While preserving the artifacts of the past, Vesterheim is firmly dedicated to nurturing a living folk heritage, offering more than forty-five classes in traditional Norwegian crafts through its Handwork School and Academy, with more than 350 participants annually. Vesterheim hosts Elderhostel programs on genealogy, folk art, and other museum themes each year. In addition, Vesterheim holds national juried exhibitions in traditional knife-making, rosemaling, weaving, and woodcarving. Vesterheim supports a full calendar of exhibitions and events with a staff of forty and an additional 450 volunteers. The museum plays a major role in Decorah's annual celebration of Scandinavian heritage, Nordic Fest, on the last full weekend in July. The exhibition schedule, calendar of events and classes, hours and admission prices, and membership information are all located on the website at www.vesterheim.org.

continued

Vesterheim is particularly proud of its collection of artifacts relating to the culinary arts. The images of Norwegian silver shown throughout this publication are all selected from the permanent collections at Vesterheim. In addition, Vesterheim's collection of wooden, metal, porcelain, and ceramic cooking utensils and serving pieces is among the great strengths of its collections, demonstrating clearly that the persistence of culinary heritage is one of the most important immigrant traditions.

List of Recipes

This Hanseatic beaker was made in Bergen in 1780.

Vesterheim: Gift of the Rebecca Shepherd estate

BOOKS BY MAIL Penfield Stocking Stuffers: You may mix titles. Retail for $6.95 each or postpaid: One book for $10.95; 2 for $18; 3 for $25; 4 for $30; 6 for $45; 12 for $80. Complete catalog of all titles $2.50. *(Prices and availability subject to change.)* Please call 1-800-728-9998.

Æbleskiver and More (Danish)
Dandy Dutch Recipes
Dutch Style Recipes
Dear Danish Recipes
Fine Finnish Foods
German Style Recipes
Great German Recipes
Norwegian Recipes
Scandinavian Holiday Recipes
Scandinavian Smorgasbord Recipes
Scandinavian Style Fish and Seafood Recipes
Scandinavian Sweet Treats
Splendid Swedish Recipes
Time-Honored Norwegian Recipes
Waffles, Flapjacks, Pancakes
Slavic Specialties
Pleasing Polish Recipes
Cherished Czech Recipes

Czech & Slovak Kolaches & Sweet Treats
Quality Czech Mushroom Recipes
Quality Dumpling Recipes
Amish Mennonite Recipes & Traditions
American Gothic Cookbook
Recipes from Ireland
Recipes from Old Mexico
Savory Scottish Recipes
Ukrainian Recipes
Tales from Texas Tables

License to Cook Series:
Italian Style;
Alaska Style; Arizona Style;
Iowa Style; Minnesota Style;
New Mexico Style; Oregon Style;
Texas Style; Wisconsin Style

PENFIELD BOOKS • 215 BROWN STREET • IOWA CITY, IA 52245-5801 • WWW.PENFIELDBOOKS.COM

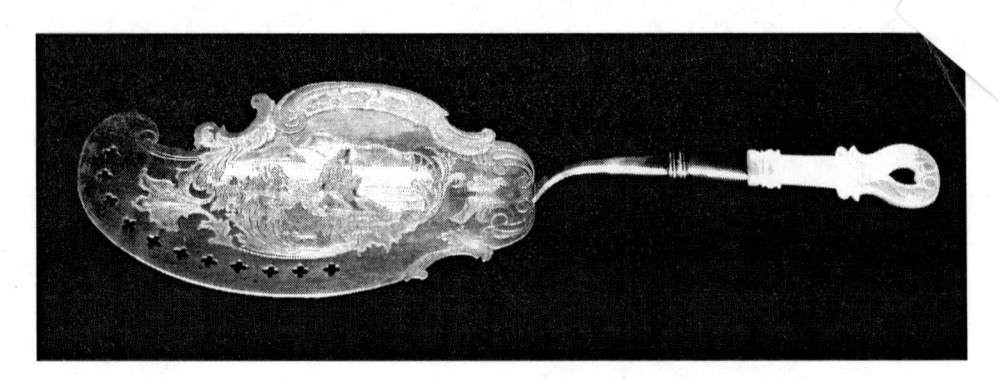

This fish server, made in Trondheim, features a mother-of-pearl handle.

Vesterheim: William O. Johnson Collection, Gift of Leslie Millholin, Jr.